Kellogg's® RICE KRISPIES®

THE RICE KRISPIES TREATS® COOKBOOK

Kellogg's®

RICE KRISPIES®

THE RICE KRISPIES TREATS® COOKBOOK

weldon**owen**

Table of Contents

Welcome to a World of Memories...

...both happy memories from the past and wonderful memories yet to come!

That's what happens when grownups and children cook together: They create not only delicious food but also delightful moments that will always be remembered and cherished.

No wonder Kellogg's Rice Krispies Treats have been making memories since 1940.

It all started when a team in the Home Economics Department at Kellogg in Battle Creek, Michigan, developed a recipe for a no-bake cookie-candy made with Rice Krispies, the popular toasted rice cereal that was introduced in 1928. Introduced on the side of the Rice Krispies cereal box, the recipe for "Krispies Marshmallow Squares," as they were first named, became hugely popular practically overnight.

Newspapers across the country reprinted the recipe. Moms everywhere wrote to Kellogg's to say how much they and their families loved the easy Rice Krispies Treats recipe, as they eventually came to be called. They became favorites in school lunch boxes. They starred at community bake sales. Making Rice Krispies Treats became one of the most popular after-school, weekend, rainy day, or holiday activities.

Why are Rice Krispies Treats so widely loved? There's the yummy taste, of course, combining toasted rice and sweet marshmallow. And who can forget that crunchy, gooey texture?

But there's more. Rice Krispies Treats are so easy and fun to make that they invite parents and kids alike to get imaginative with the recipe: to add other ingredients, shape the mixture by hand or with cookie cutters, decorate the snacks with frosting or icing or candy, and use them as a starting point for all sorts of other fun, tasty creations.

That's the reason behind this book. It shares kitchen-tested recipes for 40 different delicious, beautiful versions of Rice Krispies Treats—plus dozens more ideas to inspire you to make your own variations.

Along the way, you'll also find instructions and photos that will help guide parents and children alike in how to make, shape, and decorate their own Rice Krispies Treats—and how to pack them as gifts that family and friends will love. And special pictures from the Kellogg Archives in Battle Creek add extra touches of history and fun to these pages, including the beloved Rice Krispies characters Snap, Crackle, and Pop.

We wish you many happy memories to come as you make your own Rice Krispies Treats!

Why Use Kellogg's® Rice Krispies®?

As the first crisped rice cereal, *Kellogg's Rice Krispies* has been bringing families together in the kitchen for nearly 80 years. The "cereal that talks" captivates grownups and kids alike, and the classic taste has become one of life's simple pleasures. To experience the timeless toasted rice flavor and crunchy texture at its finest, make your *Rice Krispies Treats* only with the original *Rice Krispies* brand cereal.

Original Rice Krispies Treats®

Preparation Time: 10 minutes / Total Time: 30 minutes / Servings: 12

Here's the recipe that started it all for the no-bake sweet snack loved by kids and adults alike.

INGREDIENTS

3 tablespoons butter or margarine

1 package (10 oz., about 40) regular marshmallows

- or -

4 cups miniature marshmallows

6 cups *Rice Krispies* cereal

1. In large saucepan melt butter over low heat. Add marshmallows and stir until completely melted (*photo A, right*). Remove from heat.

2. Add KELLOGG'S RICE KRISPIES cereal (*photo C, right*). Stir until well coated.

3. Using buttered spatula or wax paper evenly press mixture into 13 x 9 x 2-inch pan coated with cooking spray. Cool. Cut into 2-inch squares (*photo D, right*). Best if served the same day.

MICROWAVE DIRECTIONS: In microwave-safe bowl heat butter and marshmallows on HIGH for 3 minutes, stirring after 2 minutes. Stir until smooth. Follow steps 2 and 3 above. Microwave cooking times may vary.

NUTRITION FACTS: **Serving Size:** 2 Squares (35g); **Calories:** 140; Calories from Fat: 25; **Total Fat:** 3g; **Saturated Fat:** 0.5g; **Trans Fat:** 0g; Cholesterol: 0mg; **Sodium:** 110mg; **Total Carbohydrate:** 27g; Dietary Fiber: 0g; **Sugars:** 13g; **Protein:** 1g.

Tips!
- For best results, use fresh marshmallows.
- 1 jar (7 oz.) marshmallow crème can be substituted for marshmallows.
- Diet, reduced calorie, or tub margarine is not recommended.
- Store no more than 2 days at room temperature in airtight container. To freeze, place in layers separated by wax paper in airtight container. Freeze for up to 6 weeks. Let stand at room temperature for 15 minutes before serving.

Safe Cooking with Kids

Before you get started with any of the recipes in this book, look over these tips to make sure everyone has a fun and safe cooking experience.

Before You Start:

- Tie back long hair, roll up loose sleeves, and cover clothes with an apron.
- Wash hands thoroughly with soap and water, and dry them before handling food.
- Keep clean, dry oven mitts or hot pads handy nearby for safe handling of hot pans, pots, and bowls.
- Keep a first-aid kit handy in the kitchen.
- Keep emergency phone numbers near the phone.

During and After Cooking:

- When cooking on the stove, point handles toward the back of the stove to prevent spills.
- Clean up spills immediately, to prevent slipping.
- Always turn off the stove burners and the oven as soon as you finish cooking.

Adult Supervision Required:

- Reading the entire recipe before beginning to cook.
- Using the stove, oven, or microwave.
- Handling hot pans, pots, and bowls.
- Using electrical appliances such as can openers.
- Cutting or slicing food with knives *(photo D, left)*.
- Handling hot water.

2-to-3-year-olds can:

- Help gather together ingredients.
- Name and count foods.

3-to-4-year-olds can:

- Mix dry ingredients together.
- Shape foods.
- Pour premeasured ingredients.

4-year-olds and up can:

- Open packages.
- Help measure ingredients *(photo B, left)*.
- Pour ingredients *(photo C, left)*.
- Press cookie cutters into *Rice Krispies Treats*.
- Shape cooled *Rice Krispies Treats* mixture by hand.
- Set the table.
- Wipe up after cooking

How to Get Creative with Rice Krispies Treats®

The delicious basic recipe for original Rice Krispies Treats *(page 8)* is also just the starting point for all kinds of other exciting recipes. Here are some of the basic ways in which you can get creative with Rice Krispies Treats.

Mix in Other Ingredients

When you stir the Rice Krispies cereal into the melted marshmallow mixture, add other small pieces of delicious ingredients such as chocolate chips, roasted shelled nuts, shredded coconut, raisins, dried or candied fruit *(page 49)*. You can also flavor and color the mixture with a little bit of sweet spices like cinnamon or nutmeg *(page 16)*, or with your favorite flavor of powdered instant pudding and pie filling mix *(page 12)*. Or just spread your favorite ingredient in the bottom of the pan before pressing in the Rice Krispies Treats mixture *(page 15)*. You can even try substituting Kellogg's Cocoa Krispies cereal for some or all of the Rice Krispies cereal!

Mold the Mixture by Hand

After you've stirred in the Rice Krispies cereal, let the mixture stand briefly until it is cool enough to handle safely. *(Grownups: Be sure to check the mixture yourself to make sure it isn't too hot.)* Then, shape however you like, from round balls to footballs *(page 68)*, Easter eggs *(page 31)* to turkey legs *(page 47)*.

Shape the Mixture with Cookie Cutters

Use all kinds of different cookie cutters to cut out whatever shapes you like from an unmolded pan of Rice Krispies Treats, from flowers *(page 20)* to stars *(page 24)*, hearts *(page 27)* to shamrocks *(page 28)* to all kinds of other shapes. You can also press the still-warm mixture into lightly greased cookie cutters to form the shapes. Or draw your own simple designs on sturdy cardboard and cut them out to make stencils that a grownup uses to cut out shapes such as hands for Thanksgiving turkeys *(page 47)*. *(Grownups: Look for cookie cutters with wide, sturdy plastic tops that kids will find easier and more comfortable to press into the mixture.)*

Decorate with Frosting, Icing, and Candies

As a finishing touch to your Rice Krispies Treats creations, spread store-bought colored frosting on top. Then, draw on them using store-bought icing squeezed carefully from small tubes. Finally, if you like, press small pieces of candy down into the frosting or icing to complete your own artistic, fun design.

How to Personalize & Wrap Rice Krispies Treats®

Whether they're the original recipe or your own special creations, Rice Krispies Treats make wonderful gifts for you to share with your friends and family. Everybody welcomes them!

Here are some of the basic ways you can give an extra personal touch to and wrap Rice Krispies Treats.

Add a Personal Touch

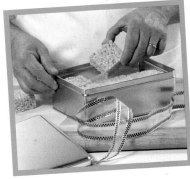

When decorating with a tube of store-bought icing, write the name of the person to whom you plan to give the Rice Krispies Treat, whether it's a Valentine's heart *(below, recipe on page 27)*, a hand-molded Mother's Day mug *(page 35)*, or a message on a birthday cake molded in a round cake pan *(page 88)*.

Tie Up Individual Snacks

For party favors or other special-occasion presents, wrap plain or decorated Rice Krispies Treats in individual cellophane bags, available from crafts and party-supply stores. After placing each one in its bag, tie a length of pretty ribbon into a bow around the opening of the bag to seal it, helping to keep the snack fresher for a longer time. *(In the photo shown here, separate batches of Rice Krispies Treats mixture have been tinted with a few drops of food coloring following the instructions in the recipe on page 27, and then molded onto wooden popsicle sticks to make Rice Krispies Treats snacks.)*

Pack into Airtight Containers

If you want to give a batch or more of Rice Krispies Treats as gifts, pack them in airtight containers that will help keep them fresher for a longer time as well as making a gift that's pretty to give and easy to wrap. Look for plain or decorative airtight metal tins in cookware stores or gift or craft shops. Use the bottom of the tin as a guide for tracing its shape onto waxed paper, cutting out several pieces along the tin's outline. Then, neatly stack the squares in layers inside the tin, separating each layer from the next with a piece of wax paper to keep them from sticking. Finally, put on the lid and wrap the tin as a present.

Banana Nut Treats™

Preparation Time: 10 minutes / Total Time: 30 minutes / Servings: 12

These all-time favorite snacks get a flavor punch from the banana pudding mix and walnut flavoring stirred into them.

INGREDIENTS

3 tablespoons butter or margarine

1 package (10 oz., about 40) regular marshmallows

- or -

4 cups miniature marshmallows

3 tablespoons banana-flavor instant pudding and pie filling

1½ teaspoons walnut extract

6 cups *Rice Krispies* cereal

For best results, see our tips on page 8.

1. In large saucepan melt butter over low heat. Add marshmallows and stir until completely melted. Remove from heat. Stir in pudding mix and walnut flavoring.

2. Add KELLOGG'S RICE KRISPIES cereal. Stir until well coated.

3. Using buttered spatula or wax paper evenly press mixture into 13 x 9 x 2-inch pan coated with cooking spray. Cool. Cut into 2-inch squares. Best if served the same day.

MICROWAVE DIRECTIONS: In microwave-safe bowl heat butter and marshmallows on HIGH for 3 minutes, stirring after 2 minutes. Stir until smooth. Add pudding mix and walnut flavoring, stirring until smooth. Follow steps 2 and 3 above. Microwave cooking times may vary.

NUTRITION FACTS: **Serving Size:** 2 Squares (39g): **Calories:** 150; Calories from Fat: 25; **Total Fat:** 3g; **Saturated Fat:** 0.5g; **Trans Fat:** 0g; **Cholesterol:** 0mg; **Sodium:** 160mg; **Total Carbohydrate:** 30g; **Dietary Fiber:** 0g; **Sugars:** 16g; **Protein:** 1g.

Mix Up the Flavor with Instant Pudding Mix!

Just a little powder from your favorite flavor of store-bought instant pudding mix, stirred in after the marshmallows have melted, adds big flavor to *Rice Krispies Treats*. Try these variations:

- **Butterscotch** *Treats:* Use 3 tablespoons butterscotch pudding mix.
- **Chocolate Fudge** *Treats:* Use 3 tablespoons rich chocolate flavor pudding mix.
- **Lemony** *Treats:* Use 3 tablespoons lemon-flavored pudding mix.

Confetti Treats™

Preparation Time: 10 minutes / Total Time: 30 minutes / Servings: 12

Multicolored candy pieces make these irresistible squares perfect for a celebration, whether you enjoy them at a birthday or a tea party.

INGREDIENTS

½ cup miniature candy-coated semisweet chocolate pieces

3 tablespoons butter or margarine

1 package (10 oz., about 40) regular marshmallows
- *or* -
4 cups miniature marshmallows

6 cups *Rice Krispies* cereal

For best results, see our tips on page 8.

1. Coat 13 x 9 x 2-inch pan with cooking spray. Evenly sprinkle candy on bottom of pan. Set aside.

2. In large saucepan melt butter over low heat. Add marshmallows and stir until completely melted. Remove from heat.

3. Add KELLOGG'S RICE KRISPIES cereal. Stir until well coated.

4. Using buttered spatula or wax paper evenly press mixture over candy in pan. Cool. Cut into 2-inch squares. Serve candy side up. Best if served the same day.

MICROWAVE DIRECTIONS: Follow step 1 above. In microwave-safe bowl heat butter and marshmallows on HIGH for 3 minutes, stirring after 2 minutes. Stir until smooth. Follow steps 3 and 4 above. Microwave cooking times may vary.

NUTRITION FACTS: Serving Size: 2 Squares (45g): Calories: 180; Calories from Fat: 45; Total Fat: 5g; Saturated Fat: 2g; Trans Fat: 0g; Cholesterol: 0mg; Sodium: 115mg; Total Carbohydrate: 33g; Dietary Fiber: 0g; Sugars: 19g; Protein: 2g.

serve Marshmallow Treats made with MARSHMALLOWS and Kellogg's RICE KRISPIES

Have a party ...GET 25¢ REFUND See Special RICE KRISPIES Package

Go Topsy-Turvy with Candy Toppings!

It's easy to make candy-topped *Treats* by spreading a layer of candy at the bottom of the pan in which you shape and mold the mixture. Try other candies the same way:

- **Gooey Gumdrop *Treats*:** Use your favorite flavor, or a mixture, of gumdrops.
- **Gummy *Treats*:** Try small gummy bears, making sure to place them face-down in the pan so they'll be face-up when you unmold the snacks.
- **Peppermint Crunch *Treats*:** Spread crushed peppermint candies or peppermint sticks in the bottom of the pan.

Spicy Raisin Treats™

Preparation Time: 10 minutes / Total Time: 30 minutes / Servings: 12

Try this new autumn-inspired twist on the original recipe, which adds pumpkin pie spice and raisins for a snack that's perfect for the holiday season.

INGREDIENTS

3 tablespoons butter or margarine

1 package (10 oz., about 40) regular marshmallows

- or -

4 cups miniature marshmallows

1 teaspoon pumpkin pie spice

6 cups *Rice Krispies* cereal

½ cup raisins

For best results, see our tips on page 8.

1. In large saucepan melt butter over low heat. Add marshmallows and stir until completely melted. Remove from heat. Stir in spice.

2. Add KELLOGG'S RICE KRISPIES cereal and raisins. Stir until well coated.

3. Using buttered spatula or wax paper evenly press mixture into 13 x 9 x 2-inch pan coated with cooking spray. Cool. Cut into 2-inch squares. Best if served the same day.

MICROWAVE DIRECTIONS: In microwave-safe bowl heat butter and marshmallows on HIGH for 3 minutes, stirring after 2 minutes. Add spice. Stir until smooth. Follow steps 2 and 3 above. Microwave cooking times may vary.

NUTRITION FACTS: **Serving Size:** 2 Squares (42g); **Calories:** 160; Calories from Fat: 25; Total Fat: 3g; Saturated Fat: 0.5g; Trans Fat: 0g; Cholesterol: 0mg; Sodium: 110mg; Total Carbohydrate: 32g; Dietary Fiber: 0g; Sugars: 18g; Protein: 2g.

Stir in Flavorful Tidbits!

Add to original recipe *(page 8)* other goodies you love.

- **Cherry** *Treats* *(left)*: Stir into the melted marshmallows 2 teaspoons cherry flavoring and, for pink color if you like, 1 teaspoon red food coloring. Add ½ cup tart dried cherries along with the *Rice Krispies* cereal.
- **Cherry Coconut** *Treats*: Along with the *Rice Krispies* cereal, stir in 1 cup flaked coconut and ½ cup well-drained and chopped maraschino cherries.
- **Raisin Peanut Butter** *Treats*: Stir ¼ cup peanut butter into the melted marshmallows. Add 1 cup raisins along with the *Rice Krispies* cereal.

Cocoa Krispies® Marshmallow Treats™

Preparation Time: 10 minutes / Total Time: 30 minutes / Servings: 12

Grownups and children alike love this variation on the original recipe *(page 8)* starring **Kellogg's Cocoa Krispies** cereal.

INGREDIENTS

3 tablespoons butter or margarine

1 package (10 oz., about 40) regular marshmallows
- or -
4 cups miniature marshmallows

6 cups *Cocoa Krispies* cereal

For best results, see our tips on page 8.

1. In large saucepan melt butter over low heat. Add marshmallows and stir until completely melted. Remove from heat.

2. Add KELLOGG'S COCOA KRISPIES cereal. Stir until well coated.

3. Using buttered spatula or wax paper evenly press mixture into 13 x 9 x 2-inch pan coated with cooking spray. Cool. Cut into 2-inch squares. Best if served the same day.

MICROWAVE DIRECTIONS: In microwave-safe bowl heat butter and marshmallows on HIGH for 3 minutes, stirring after 2 minutes. Stir until smooth. Follow steps 2 and 3 above. Microwave cooking times may vary.

NUTRITION FACTS: Serving Size: 2 Squares (43g): Calories: 170; Calories from Fat: 30; Total Fat: 3.5g; Saturated Fat: 1g; Trans Fat: 0g; Cholesterol: 0mg; Sodium: 125mg; Total Carbohydrate: 33g; Dietary Fiber: 0g; Sugars: 19g; Protein: 1g.

Try More Chocolatey Treats™!

If you love chocolate, as so many people do, try these other great variations.

- **Chewy Chocolate *Treats*:** Start with the original recipe *(page 8)* and stir into the melted marshmallows 2 tablespoons unsweetened cocoa powder and 1 teaspoon chocolate flavoring before adding the *Rice Krispies* cereal.
- **Chocolate Mint *Treats*:** Following the ingredients and instructions for *Chewy Chocolate Treats*, add to the melted marshmallows 1½ teaspoons peppermint flavoring.
- **Marbled *Treats*:** Following the original recipe *(page 8)*, substitute *Kellogg's Cocoa Krispies* cereal for half of the *Rice Krispies* cereal.

Rice Krispies Treats® Flowers

Preparation Time: 20 minutes / Total Time: 40 minutes / Servings: 12

Any flower-shaped cookie cutter and some ready-to-use frosting turn everyone's favorite snacks into pretty springtime delights.

INGREDIENTS

3 tablespoons butter or margarine

1 package (10 oz., about 40) regular marshmallows
- *or* -
4 cups miniature marshmallows

6 cups *Rice Krispies* cereal

Canned frosting

Assorted candies

For best results, see our tips on page 8.

1. In large saucepan melt butter over low heat. Add marshmallows and stir until completely melted. Remove from heat.

2. Add KELLOGG'S RICE KRISPIES cereal. Stir until well coated.

3. Using buttered spatula or wax paper evenly press mixture into 15 x 10 x 1-inch pan coated with cooking spray. Cool slightly. Using cookie cutters coated with cooking spray cut into flower shapes. Decorate with frosting and/or candies. Best if served the same day.

MICROWAVE DIRECTIONS: In microwave-safe bowl heat butter and marshmallows on HIGH for 3 minutes, stirring after 2 minutes. Stir until smooth. Follow steps 2 and 3 above. Microwave cooking times may vary.

NUTRITION FACTS: **Serving Size:** 1 Flower, undecorated (35g); **Calories:** 140; **Calories from Fat:** 25; **Total Fat:** 3g; **Saturated Fat:** 0.5g; **Trans Fat:** 0g; **Cholesterol:** 0mg; **Sodium:** 110mg; **Total Carbohydrate:** 27g; **Dietary Fiber:** 0g; **Sugars:** 13g; **Protein:** 1g.

Find Inspiration in Nature!

The beauty of the natural world offers us all kinds of great ideas for shaping and decorating *Rice Krispies Treats*. Use shaped cookie cutters, or stencils that you draw and cut out from sturdy cardboard. *(With stencils, a grownup should cut out the shapes.)*

- **Butterflies** *(left):* Use a butterfly cookie cutter and add realistic or playful decorations.
- **Autumn Leaves:** Cut out leaves and frost or ice with fall colors of gold, red, and brown.
- **Fish:** Use fish-shaped cutters or stencils and decorate with eyes, fins, and even scales using frosting, gel, and candies.

Funny Faces

Preparation Time: 20 minutes / Total Time: 40 minutes / Servings: 12

With frosting, candies, and your imagination, you can have fun transforming your favorite snacks into all kinds of funny faces.

INGREDIENTS

3 tablespoons butter or margarine

1 package (10 oz., about 40) regular marshmallows
- or -
4 cups miniature marshmallows

Food colorings (optional)

6 cups *Rice Krispies* cereal
- or -
6 cups *Cocoa Krispies* cereal

Canned frosting or decorating gel

Assorted candies

For best results, see our tips on page 8.

1. In large saucepan melt butter over low heat. Add marshmallows and stir until completely melted. Remove from heat. To turn the mixture a fun color, stir in a few drops of food coloring, if desired.

2. Add KELLOGG'S RICE KRISPIES cereal. Stir until well coated.

3. Using ½-cup measuring cup coated with cooking spray divide warm cereal mixture into portions. Using buttered hands shape each portion into a circular shape. Decorate with frosting and/or candies. Best if served the same day.

MICROWAVE DIRECTIONS: In microwave-safe bowl heat butter and marshmallows on HIGH for 3 minutes, stirring after 2 minutes. Stir until smooth. To tint a color, stir in a few drops of food coloring, if desired. Follow steps 2 and 3 above. Microwave cooking times may vary.

NUTRITION FACTS: **Serving Size:** 1 Funny Face, undecorated (35g): **Calories:** 140; **Calories from Fat:** 25; **Total Fat:** 3g; **Saturated Fat:** 0.5g; **Trans Fat:** 0g; **Cholesterol:** 0mg; **Sodium:** 110mg; **Total Carbohydrate:** 27g; **Dietary Fiber:** 0g; **Sugars:** 13g; **Protein:** 1g.

Have a Decorating Contest!

Turn decorating *Rice Krispies Treats* into a game or activity for parties or other get-togethers. Cover a table with craft paper or a paper tablecloth and top with cut-out shapes and decorating ingredients. Demonstrate how to decorate, let everyone go wild, and then vote on the winners. *(Grownups: Have great prizes ready for everyone!)* Have cellophane bags and ribbons ready *(page 11)* for guests who want to take their creations home instead of eating them on the spot.

Star Treats™

Preparation Time: 20 minutes / Total Time: 40 minutes / Servings: 12

Celebrate life's little successes with these easy stars, which you can have fun decorating to make your own stellar works of edible art!

INGREDIENTS

3 tablespoons butter or margarine

1 package (10 oz., about 40) regular marshmallows

- or -

4 cups miniature marshmallows

6 cups *Rice Krispies* cereal

Canned frosting or decorating gel

Assorted candies or multicolored sprinkles

For best results, see our tips on page 8.

1. In large saucepan melt butter over low heat. Add marshmallows and stir until completely melted. Remove from heat.

2. Add KELLOGG'S RICE KRISPIES cereal. Stir until well coated.

3. Using buttered spatula or wax paper evenly press mixture into 15 x 10 x 1-inch pan coated with cooking spray. Cool slightly. Using cookie cutter coated with cooking spray cut into star shapes. Decorate with frosting and/or candies. Best if served the same day.

MICROWAVE DIRECTIONS: In microwave-safe bowl heat butter and marshmallows on HIGH for 3 minutes, stirring after 2 minutes. Stir until smooth. Follow steps 2 and 3 above. Microwave cooking times may vary.

NUTRITION FACTS: Serving Size: 1 Star, undecorated (35g): Calories: 140; Calories from Fat: 25; Total Fat: 3g; Saturated Fat: 0.5g; Trans Fat: 0g; Cholesterol: 0mg; Sodium: 110mg; Total Carbohydrate: 27g; Dietary Fiber: 0g; Sugars: 13g; Protein: 1g.

Reach for the Sky!

You can find all sorts of *Rice Krispies Treats* inspirations by looking into the sky.

- **Suns:** Cut out round shapes and coat with yellow frosting. Use white or red gel to draw the sun's rays around the edges—and maybe add a smiley face!
- **Rainbows:** Use an arc-shaped cardboard stencil to cut out rainbow shapes. *(Grownups: This is a job for you.)* Then, in frosting, add rainbow colors.
- **Birds:** Cut out bird shapes with a cookie cutter or stencil and make beaks, eyes, and feathers with frosting, icing, and candies.

Valentine Heart Cut-outs

Preparation Time: 20 minutes / Total Time: 40 minutes / Servings: 12

Make Valentine's Day more memorable by giving the special people in your life these colorful hearts.

INGREDIENTS

3 tablespoons butter or margarine

1 package (10 oz., about 40) marshmallows
- or -
4 cups miniature marshmallows

Food coloring (optional)

6 cups *Rice Krispies* cereal

Canned frosting or decorating gel

For best results, see our tips on page 8.

1. In large saucepan melt butter over low heat. Add marshmallows and stir until completely melted. Stir in food coloring (if desired). Remove from heat.

2. Add KELLOGG'S RICE KRISPIES cereal. Stir until well coated.

3. Using buttered spatula or wax paper evenly press mixture into 13 x 9 x 2-inch pan coated with cooking spray. Cool slightly. Using cookie cutters coated with cooking spray cut into desired shapes. Decorate with frosting and/or candies. Best if served the same day.

MICROWAVE DIRECTIONS: In microwave-safe bowl heat butter and marshmallows on HIGH for 3 minutes, stirring after 2 minutes. Stir until smooth. Follow steps 2 and 3 above. Microwave cooking times may vary.

NUTRITION FACTS: Serving Size: 1 Heart, undecorated (35g): Calories: 140; Calories from Fat: 25; Total Fat: 3g; Saturated Fat: 0.5g; Trans Fat: 0g; Cholesterol: 0mg; Sodium: 110mg; Total Carbohydrate: 27g; Dietary Fiber: 0g; Sugars: 13g; Protein: 1g.

Deliver a Valentine's Greeting!

Instead of coloring, cutting out, and decorating Valentine Hearts, you could also give your Valentine a whole pan-sized **Valentine's Day Greeting** *(right)*. To make the special delight, simply make the original recipe *(page 8)* in a 13 x 9 x 2-inch pan. When the mixture has cooled, unmold onto a flat serving platter or tray. Using red, pink, and white frosting, decorating gel, and candies, add a heart, a message, and other pretty decorations.

St. Patrick's Day Shamrocks

Preparation Time: 20 minutes / Total Time: 40 minutes / Servings: 12

When you serve these clover- shaped delights to your guests on March 17, they'll dance an Irish jig of happiness.

INGREDIENTS

3 tablespoons butter or margarine

1 package (10 oz. about 40) regular marshmallows

- or -

4 cups miniature marshmallows

6 cups *Rice Krispies* cereal

Canned frosting or decorating gel

Green decorating sugar (optional)

For best results, see our tips on page 8.

1. In large saucepan melt butter over low heat. Add marshmallows and stir until completely melted. Remove from heat.

2. Add KELLOGG'S RICE KRISPIES cereal. Stir until well coated.

3. Using buttered spatula or wax paper evenly press mixture into 13 x 9 x 2-inch pan coated with cooking spray. Cool slightly. Using cookie cutter coated with cooking spray cut into shamrocks. Decorate with frosting and decorating sugar (if desired). Best if served the same day.

MICROWAVE DIRECTIONS: In microwave-safe bowl heat butter and marshmallows on HIGH for 3 minutes, stirring after 2 minutes. Stir until smooth. Follow steps 2 and 3 above. Microwave cooking times may vary.

NUTRITION FACTS: **Serving Size:** 1 Shamrock (40g): **Calories:** 160; Calories from Fat: 25; **Total Fat:** 3g; **Saturated Fat:** 2g; **Trans Fat:** 0g; **Cholesterol:** 10mg; **Sodium:** 120mg; **Total Carbohydrate:** 31g; **Dietary Fiber:** 0g; **Sugars:** 15g; **Protein:** 1g.

Celebrate the Luck o' the Irish!

St. Patrick's Day, celebrated each year on March 17, offers lots of opportunities to make imaginative *Rice Krispies Treats*.

- **Green *Treats*:** Stir a few drops of green food coloring into the melted marshmallows to tint your *Treats* the favorite Irish color.
- **Irish Flags:** Decorate flag shapes with vertical bars of green, white, and orange.
- **Pots o' Gold:** Use a stencil to cut out shapes like leprechauns' magical pots. *(Grownups: This is a job for you.)* Cover with gold-colored frosting and decorate the tops with decorating gel or small disc-shaped candies to look like gold coins.

Easter Egg Treats™

Preparation Time: 20 minutes / Total Time: 40 minutes / Servings: 18

There's no need to hunt for Easter eggs when you greet guests with these delights. Or shape and decorate them as part of your Easter party!

INGREDIENTS

3 tablespoons butter or margarine

1 package (10 oz., about 40) regular marshmallows

- or -

4 cups miniature marshmallows

6 cups *Rice Krispies* cereal

- or -

6 cups *Cocoa Krispies* cereal

Canned frosting or decorating gel

Assorted candies

For best results, see our tips on page 8.

1. In large saucepan melt butter over low heat. Add marshmallows and stir until completely melted. Remove from heat.

2. Add KELLOGG'S RICE KRISPIES cereal. Stir until well coated.

3. Using ⅓-cup measuring cup coated with cooking spray divide warm cereal mixture into portions. Using buttered hands shape each portion into egg shape. Cool. Decorate with frosting and/or candies. Best if served the same day.

MICROWAVE DIRECTIONS: In microwave-safe bowl heat butter and marshmallows on HIGH for 3 minutes, stirring after 2 minutes. Stir until smooth. Follow steps 2 and 3 above. Microwave cooking times may vary.

NUTRITION FACTS: Serving Size: 1 Egg, undecorated (35g): Calories: 140; Calories from Fat: 25; Total Fat: 3g; Saturated Fat: 0.5g; Trans Fat: 0g; Cholesterol: 0mg; Sodium: 110mg; Total Carbohydrate: 27g; Dietary Fiber: 0g; Sugars: 13g; Protein: 1g.

Hunt for More Fun Easter Egg Ideas!

Instead of decorating molded **Easter Egg Treats** with frosting, try dipping them in chocolate *(left)*. Form egg shapes by hand as directed in the recipe above, or shape inside plastic snap-apart Easter eggs coated with cooking spray. When they're cool, melt together 1½ cups semisweet or milk chocolate morsels and 5 teaspoons shortening in a small saucepan over low heat, stirring constantly. *(Grownups: This is a job for you.)* Dip the bottoms of the eggs into the chocolate, decorate with multicolored sprinkles if you like, place on a wax-paper-lined baking sheet, and refrigerate until set.

Chocolate Bunny Treats™

Preparation Time: 20 minutes / Total Time: 40 minutes / Servings: 4

To flavor this funny bunny, we added chocolate chips to the original recipe *(page 8)*. Then, we used simple round cookie cutters to shape it.

INGREDIENTS

1 cup (6 oz.) semisweet chocolate morsels

3 tablespoons butter or margarine

1 package (10 oz., about 40) marshmallows
- or -
4 cups miniature marshmallows

6 cups *Rice Krispies* cereal

Canned frosting or decorating gel

Assorted candies

For best results, see our tips on page 8.

1. In large saucepan melt chocolate morsels and butter over low heat. Add marshmallows and stir until completely melted. Remove from heat.

2. Add KELLOGG'S RICE KRISPIES cereal. Stir until well coated.

3. Using buttered spatula or wax paper evenly press mixture into 15 x 10 x 1-inch pan coated with cooking spray. Cool slightly.

4. Using large circle cookie cutter, very small circle cookie cutter and rabbit head cookie cutter coated with cooking spray cut cereal mixture into shapes. For each rabbit, attach one rabbit head shape to top of large circle shape with frosting. Attach one small circle for tail to each. Decorate with frosting and/or candies. Best if served the same day.

MICROWAVE DIRECTIONS: In microwave-safe bowl heat chocolate morsels, butter and marshmallows on HIGH for 3 minutes, stirring after 2 minutes. Stir until smooth. Follow steps 2, 3, and 4 above. Microwave cooking times may vary.

NUTRITION FACTS: Serving Size: 1 Bunny (149g): Calories: 620; Calories from Fat: 190; Total Fat: 21g; Saturated Fat: 9g; Trans Fat: 1.5g; Cholesterol: 0mg; Sodium: 320mg; Total Carbohydrate: 108g; Dietary Fiber: 2g; Sugars: 63g; Protein: 6g.

Hop to It Making Hand-molded Bunnies!

Try molding **Easter Bunny** *Treats* by hand. Prepare the original recipe *(page 8)* and divide the warm cereal mixture into portions using a ⅓-cup measuring cup coated with cooking spray. Using clean buttered hands, shape into balls. With frosting, attach two balls together to form a body and head. With frosting, attach ears cut from construction paper. Decorate with frosting and candies.

Mother's Day Mug

Preparation Time: 20 minutes / Total Time: 40 minutes / Servings: 4

Make Mom a yummy mug for Mother's Day. It won't hold coffee or tea, but it sure tastes great.

INGREDIENTS

3 tablespoons butter or margarine

1 package (10 oz., about 40) regular marshmallows

- or -

4 cups miniature marshmallows

6 cups *Rice Krispies* cereal

Canned frosting or decorating gel

For best results, see our tips on page 8.

1. In large saucepan melt butter over low heat. Add marshmallows and stir until completely melted. Remove from heat.

2. Add KELLOGG'S RICE KRISPIES cereal. Stir until well coated.

3. Cool slightly. Using buttered hands shape cereal mixture into mug shapes, reserving small portions of cereal mixture for handles. Attach one handle to each mug, securing with frosting. Decorate with additional frosting. Best if served the same day.

MICROWAVE DIRECTIONS: In microwave-safe bowl heat butter and marshmallows on HIGH for 3 minutes, stirring after 2 minutes. Stir until smooth. Follow steps 2 and 3 above. Microwave cooking times may vary.

NUTRITION FACTS: Serving Size: 1 Mug (106g): Calories: 410; Calories from Fat: 80; Total Fat: 8g; Saturated Fat: 1.5g; Trans Fat: 0g; Cholesterol: 0mg; Sodium: 320mg; Total Carbohydrate: 81g; Dietary Fiber: 0g; Sugars: 39g; Protein: 4g.

"Mother, did you say *Kellogg's* ?"

Give Mom Some of Her Favorite Treats™!

Instead of making a mug for Mom, think about some of her other favorite things and use them as inspiration for creating other special *Treats*.

- **Bouquet of *Treats*:** Along with fresh-cut blossoms or a plant, give Mom a plateful of beautifully decorated *Rice Krispies Treats* Flowers *(page 20)*.
- **Funny Faces** *(page 23)*: Give Mom a big smile with an assortment of silly snacks.
- **Mother's Day Greeting Card:** Follow the instructions for the **Valentine's Greeting** *(page 27)*, decorating it instead as a giant Mother's Day card.

Father's Day Shirt and Tie

Preparation Time: 20 minutes / Total Time: 40 minutes / Servings: 6

Give your dad his favorite kind of shirt and tie as a Father's Day present. He'll enjoy every bite!

INGREDIENTS

3 tablespoons butter or margarine

1 package (10 oz., about 40) regular marshmallows
- or -
4 cups miniature marshmallows

6 cups *Rice Krispies* cereal

Canned frosting

For best results, see our tips on page 8.

1. In large saucepan melt butter over low heat. Add marshmallows and stir until completely melted. Remove from heat.

2. Add KELLOGG'S RICE KRISPIES cereal. Stir until well coated.

3. Using buttered spatula or wax paper evenly press mixture into 13 x 9 x 2-inch pan coated with cooking spray. Cool. Using canned frosting pipe tie and shirt collar on top. To serve cut into 2-inch squares. Best if served the same day.

MICROWAVE DIRECTIONS: In microwave-safe bowl heat butter and marshmallows on HIGH for 3 minutes, stirring after 2 minutes. Stir until smooth. Follow steps 2 and 3 above. Microwave cooking times may vary.

NUTRITION FACTS: **Serving Size:** 2 Squares, undecorated (35g): **Calories:** 140; **Calories from Fat:** 25; **Total Fat:** 3g; **Saturated Fat:** 0.5g; **Trans Fat:** 0g; **Cholesterol:** 0mg; **Sodium:** 110mg; **Total Carbohydrate:** 27g; **Dietary Fiber:** 0g; **Sugars:** 13g; **Protein:** 1g.

Treat Dad to a Father's Day He Won't Forget!

If your dad isn't a shirt-and-tie kind of guy, think about other things he might like.
- **Hobbies:** Does Dad collect stamps, or does he love to fish? Both hobbies suggest fun ideas for imaginatively shaped and decorated *Treats*.
- **Remote Control** *Treats (left)*: If he loves to channel-surf, make Dad a pan of *Treats* using *Rice Krispies* cereal or *Cocoa Krispies* cereal and decorate it like a TV remote control with frosting and candies for the buttons.
- **Sports-themed** *Treats*: Create snacks inspired by his favorite sports, such as **Soccer Balls and Baseballs** *(page 67)* or **Chocolate Nutty Mini-Footballs** *(page 68)*.

Flag Treats™

Preparation Time: 20 minutes / Total Time: 40 minutes / Servings: 8

Celebrate the Fourth of July with these red, white, and blue decorated snacks.

INGREDIENTS

3 tablespoons butter or margarine

1 package (10 oz., about 40) marshmallows
- or -
4 cups miniature marshmallows

6 cups *Rice Krispies* cereal

Canned frosting or decorating gel

Assorted candies

For best results, see our tips on page 8.

1. In large saucepan melt butter over low heat. Add marshmallows and stir until completely melted. Remove from heat.

2. Add KELLOGG'S RICE KRISPIES cereal. Stir until well coated.

3. Using buttered spatula or wax paper evenly press mixture into 13 x 9 x 2-inch pan coated with cooking spray. Cool. Cut into 8 rectangles. Decorate with frosting and/or candies. Best if served the same day.

MICROWAVE DIRECTIONS: In microwave-safe bowl heat butter and marshmallows on HIGH for 3 minutes, stirring after 2 minutes. Stir until smooth. Follow steps 2 and 3 above. Microwave cooking times may vary.

NUTRITION FACTS: Serving Size: 1 Flag (53g): Calories: 210; Calories from Fat: 40; Total Fat: 4g; Saturated Fat: 1g; Trans Fat: 0.5g; Cholesterol: 0mg; Sodium: 160mg; Total Carbohydrate: 40g; Dietary Fiber: 0g; Sugars: 10g; Protein: 2g.

Salute These Other Patriotic Treats™!

With some red, white, and blue frosting, shiny candies in the same colors, and a little imagination, it's easy to come up with great snack ideas for the Fourth of July.

- **Fireworks:** Find skyrocket- or firecracker-shaped cutters.
- **Liberty Bells:** Use a bell-shaped cookie cutter and decorate with silver frosting.
- **The Number 4:** Look for this number cutter and frost in holiday colors.
- **Uncle Sam Hats:** Cut out tall hat shapes and decorate with stars and stripes.

Ghostly Snack Treats™

Preparation Time: 20 minutes / Total Time: 40 minutes / Servings: 12

> Little goblins at your house will love making and eating these spooky delights.

INGREDIENTS

3 tablespoons butter or margarine

1 package (10 oz., about 40) regular marshmallows

- or -

4 cups miniature marshmallows

6 cups *Rice Krispies* cereal

Flaked coconut

Canned frosting or decorating gel

Assorted candies

For best results, see our tips on page 8.

1. In large saucepan melt butter over low heat. Add marshmallows and stir until completely melted. Remove from heat.

2. Add KELLOGG'S RICE KRISPIES cereal. Stir until well coated.

3. Using ½-cup measuring cup coated with cooking spray divide warm cereal mixture into portions. Using buttered hands shape each portion into ghost shape. Cool. Decorate with coconut, frosting and/or candies. Best if served the same day.

MICROWAVE DIRECTIONS: In microwave-safe bowl heat butter and marshmallows on HIGH for 3 minutes, stirring after 2 minutes. Stir until smooth. Follow steps 2 and 3 above. Microwave cooking times may vary.

NUTRITION FACTS: Serving Size: 1 Ghost (35g): Calories: 140; Calories from Fat: 25; Total Fat: 3g; Saturated Fat: 0.5g; Trans Fat: 0g; Cholesterol: 0mg; Sodium: 110mg; Total Carbohydrate: 27g; Dietary Fiber: 0g; Sugars: 13g; Protein: 1g.

Scare Up Some Halloween Cats!

It's easy to shape other fun and spooky **Halloween** *Treats* like cats *(left)*, which you can make with either *Cocoa Krispies* cereal or *Rice Krispies* cereal or a combination of the two. For a batch of cats, prepare the original recipe *(page 8)*. While the cereal mixture is still warm, use a ½-cup measuring cup coated with cooking spray to divide it into portions. Using clean hands coated with butter or cooking spray, shape each portion into a ball. Decorate with candy corn, jelly beans, candy-coated chocolate pieces, and black string licorice for eyes, nose, mouth, ears, and whiskers.

Silly Halloween Monster Treats™

Preparation Time: 20 minutes / Total Time: 40 minutes / Servings: 8

Little hands make great helpers when it's time to add the funny faces to these nonscary monsters.

INGREDIENTS

3 tablespoons butter or margarine

1 package (10 oz., about 40) regular marshmallows

- or -

4 cups miniature marshmallows

6 cups *Rice Krispies* cereal

- or -

6 cups *Cocoa Krispies* cereal

Canned frosting or decorating gel

Assorted candies

For best results, see our tips on page 8.

1. In large saucepan melt butter over low heat. Add marshmallows and stir until completely melted. Remove from heat.

2. Add KELLOGG'S RICE KRISPIES cereal. Stir until well coated.

3. Using buttered spatula or wax paper evenly press mixture into 13 x 9 x 2-inch pan coated with cooking spray. Cool. Cut into 8 rectangles. Decorate with frosting and/or candies to make monster faces. Best if served the same day.

MICROWAVE DIRECTIONS: In microwave-safe bowl heat butter and marshmallows on HIGH for 3 minutes, stirring after 2 minutes. Stir until smooth. Follow steps 2 and 3 above. Microwave cooking times may vary.

NUTRITION FACTS: Serving Size: 1 Monster (71g): Calories: 270; Calories from Fat: 50; Total Fat: 6g; Saturated Fat: 1g; Trans Fat: 0g; Cholesterol: 0mg; Sodium: 220mg; Total Carbohydrate: 54g; Dietary Fiber: 0g; Sugars: 26g; Protein: 3g.

Make Tricky Snacks for Your Halloween Party!

Try a batch of **Chocolate Pumpkin Eaters** *(right)*. To make them, prepare a batch of the original recipe *(page 8)*. While the cereal mixture is still warm, use a ½-cup measuring cup coated with cooking spray to divide into portions. Using clean hands coated with butter, shape into balls. Push half of a pretzel rod stick into each. Cool. In a small saucepan over low heat, melt 1 cup semisweet chocolate morsels with 1 tablespoon shortening, stirring constantly. *(Grownups: This is a job for you.)* Hold each ball by the pretzel, dip in chocolate, decorate with sprinkles, and refrigerate on a wax-paper-lined baking sheet until set.

Cocoa Krispies® Earth Worm Treats™

Preparation Time: 10 minutes / Total Time: 40 minutes / Servings: 12

Anyone who loves things that squiggle and wiggle will find this chocolate delight perfect for a Halloween party.

INGREDIENTS

3 tablespoons butter or margarine

1 package (10 oz., about 40) regular marshmallows
- or -
4 cups miniature marshmallows

6 cups *Cocoa Krispies* cereal

1 package (2.75 oz., about 12) gummy worms

6 chocolate sandwich cookies, finely crushed (¾ cup)

For best results, see our tips on page 8.

1. In large saucepan melt butter over low heat. Add marshmallows and stir until completely melted. Remove from heat.

2. Add KELLOGG'S COCOA KRISPIES cereal. Stir until well coated.

3. Using buttered spatula or wax paper spread mixture into 13 x 9 x 2-inch pan coated with cooking spray, leaving uneven surface. (Do not press firmly.) Arrange gummy worms on top. Sprinkle with cookie crumbs, lightly pressing into cereal mixture. Cool. Cut into 12 squares. Best if served the same day.

MICROWAVE DIRECTIONS: In microwave-safe bowl heat butter and marshmallows on HIGH for 3 minutes, stirring after 2 minutes. Stir until smooth. Follow steps 2 and 3 above. Microwave cooking times may vary.

NUTRITION FACTS: Serving Size: 1 Square (56g): Calories: 220; Calories from Fat: 40; Total Fat: 4.5g; Saturated Fat: 1g; Trans Fat: 1g; Cholesterol: 0mg; Sodium: 160mg; Total Carbohydrate: 45g; Dietary Fiber: less than 1g; Sugars: 28g; Protein: 2g.

Give Your Friends More Creepy-Crawly Treats™!

It's fun to let your imagination run wild at Halloween, making *Treats* that can raise your hair and raise a smile at the same time—like these **Spider Treats** *(left)*. To make them, begin preparing the original recipe *(page 8)*, stirring a few drops of your favorite creepy food coloring into the melted marshmallow mixture before adding the *Rice Krispies* cereal. Using clean buttered hands, shape the warm mixture into 8 spiders, with small ball-shaped heads and bigger egg-shaped bodies. Decorate with frosting, candy corn, and licorice string to make eyes, fangs, legs, and spiky backs.

Thanksgiving Turkey Handprint Treats™

Preparation Time: 20 minutes / Total Time: 40 minutes / Servings: 12

Use a stencil made from the outline of your own hand, plus a little frosting and candies, to make these cheery holiday turkeys.

INGREDIENTS

3 tablespoons butter or margarine

1 package (10 oz., about 40) regular marshmallows

- or -

4 cups miniature marshmallows

6 cups *Rice Krispies* cereal

- or -

6 cups *Cocoa Krispies* cereal

Canned frosting or decorating gel

Assorted candies

For best results, see our tips on page 8.

1. Trace your handprint onto cardboard. Cut out. Set aside.

2. In large saucepan melt butter over low heat. Add marshmallows and stir until completely melted. Remove from heat.

3. Add KELLOGG'S RICE KRISPIES cereal. Stir until well coated.

4. Using buttered spatula or wax paper evenly press mixture into 15 x 10 x 1-inch pan coated with cooking spray. Cool slightly. Using knife coated with cooking spray cut around handprint pattern. Decorate with frosting and/or candies, using thumb portion of cutout for turkey head and finger portions for turkey tail feathers. Best if served the same day.

MICROWAVE DIRECTIONS: Follow step 1 above. In microwave-safe bowl heat butter and marshmallows on HIGH for 3 minutes, stirring after 2 minutes. Stir until smooth. Follow steps 3 and 4 above. Microwave cooking times may vary.

NUTRITION FACTS: Serving Size: 1 Turkey (65g): Calories: 140; Calories from Fat: 25; Total Fat: 3g; Saturated Fat: 0.5g; Trans Fat: 0g; Cholesterol: 0mg; Sodium: 110mg; Total Carbohydrate: 27g; Dietary Fiber: 0g; Sugars: 13g; Protein: 1g.

Gobble Up Some Thanksgiving Drumsticks!

Try **Turkey Drumstick** *Treats* (right) as another holiday table decoration. Make the original recipe (page 8). Let the mixture cool slightly and use clean hands coated with butter to shape 12 small drumstick shapes. Spread peanut butter on the plump "meaty" end, dip in *Cocoa Krispies* cereal, and refrigerate until firm.

Festive Fruit Wreath

Preparation Time: 20 minutes / Total Time: 40 minutes / Servings: 32

Stir dates, candied cherries, and walnuts into the original recipe *(page 8)*, and then shape the mixture into a wreath to make an edible decoration for your holiday table.

1. In large saucepan melt butter over low heat. Add marshmallows and stir until completely melted. Remove from heat. Stir in vanilla.

2. Add KELLOGG'S RICE KRISPIES cereal, dates, red cherries, green cherries and nuts. Stir until well coated.

3. Transfer cereal mixture to wax paper. Using buttered hands shape mixture into wreath approximately 8 inches in diameter. Decorate with candy and sprinkle with powdered sugar, if desired. To serve, cut into thin slices. Best if served the same day.

In microwave-safe bowl heat butter and marshmallows on HIGH for 3 minutes, stirring after 2 minutes. Stir until smooth. Add vanilla, stirring until combined. Follow steps 2 and 3 above. Microwave cooking times may vary.

Serving Size: Calories: Calories from Fat: Total Fat: Saturated Fat: Trans Fat: Cholesterol: Sodium: Total Carbohydrate: Dietary Fiber: Sugars: Protein:

INGREDIENTS

3 tablespoons butter or margarine

1 package (10 oz., about 40) regular marshmallows
- *or* -
4 cups miniature marshmallows

1 teaspoon vanilla extract

5 cups *Rice Krispies* cereal

½ cup chopped dates

½ cup chopped red candied cherries

½ cup chopped green candied cherries

½ cup broken walnuts

Multicolored candies (optional)

Powdered sugar (optional)

For best results, see our tips on page 8.

Deck the Table with Mini-Wreaths!

For another fun holiday activity, try **Mini-Wreaths Treats**. Prepare a batch of the original recipe *(page 8)*, stirring 1 teaspoon of green food coloring into the melted marshmallow mixture before adding the *Rice Krispies* cereal. Let cool slightly and use a ¼-cup measuring cup coated with cooking spray to divide into portions. With clean hands coated with butter, shape each portion into a small ring-shaped wreath and decorate with frosting and candies.

Holiday Lights Treats™

Preparation Time: 20 minutes / Total Time: 40 minutes / Servings: 15

Brighten up your holiday table with these edible "lights," easily made from the original recipe *(page 8)* plus a few drops of food coloring and string licorice.

INGREDIENTS

3 tablespoons butter or margarine

1 package (10 oz., about 40) regular marshmallows
- or -
4 cups miniature marshmallows

6 cups *Rice Krispies* cereal

Food coloring (optional)

Red or black string licorice

For best results, see our tips on page 8.

1. In large saucepan melt butter over low heat. Add marshmallows and stir until completely melted. Remove from heat. Divide marshmallow mixture into 4 or 5 portions. Stir a few drops of different food colors into each portion, if desired.

2. Divide KELLOGG'S RICE KRISPIES cereal among marshmallow portions. Stir each until well coated. Cool slightly.

3. Using buttered hands shape cereal mixtures into 14 holiday light bulbs and 1 plug. Place on wax paper.

4. Shape licorice into circle to form holiday lights wire. Attach cereal lights and plug to licorice with frosting. Best if served the same day.

MICROWAVE DIRECTIONS: In microwave-safe bowl heat butter and marshmallows on HIGH for 3 minutes, stirring after 2 minutes. Stir until smooth. Divide marshmallow mixture into 4 or 5 portions. Stir a few drops of different food colors into each portion, if desired. Follow steps 2 thru 4 above. Microwave cooking times may vary.

NUTRITION FACTS: Serving Size: 1 Light Bulb or Plug plus Licorice (28g): Calories: 110; Calories from Fat: 20; Total Fat: 2.5g; Saturated Fat: 0g; Trans Fat: 0g; Cholesterol: 0mg; Sodium: 85mg; Total Carbohydrate: 22g; Dietary Fiber: 0g; Sugars: 10g; Protein: 1g.

Enjoy a New Twist on Holiday Tradition!

For another edible Christmas decoration, turn the original recipe *(page 8)* into **Candy Cane Treats** *(left)*. Let the cereal mixture cool slightly and use clean hands coated with butter to shape 2 large canes or 12 smaller ones. Decorate each with stripes of red string licorice, secured with white frosting.

Frosted Snowman Snack Treats™

Preparation Time: 20 minutes / Total Time: 40 minutes / Servings: 12

A little frosting and some of your favorite holiday candies can turn the original recipe *(page 8)* into jaunty snowmen.

INGREDIENTS

3 tablespoons butter or margarine

1 package (10 oz., about 40) regular marshmallows
- *or* -
4 cups miniature marshmallows

6 cups *Rice Krispies* cereal
- *or* -
6 cups *Cocoa Krispies* cereal

Canned frosting or decorating gel

Assorted candies

For best results, see our tips on page 8.

1. In large saucepan melt butter over low heat. Add marshmallows and stir until completely melted. Remove from heat.

2. Add KELLOGG'S RICE KRISPIES cereal. Stir until well coated.

3. Using buttered spatula or wax paper evenly press mixture into 15 x 10 x 1-inch pan coated with cooking spray. Cool. Using 4-inch cookie cutter coated with cooking spray cut into snowman shapes. (If desired, use 2-, 1¾- and 1½-inch round cookie cutters coated with cooking spray to cut into circles.)

4. Decorate snowmen with frosting and/or candies. (If using circles, for each snowman connect three different sized circles together with frosting. Decorate with remaining frosting and/or candies.) Best if served the same day.

MICROWAVE DIRECTIONS: In microwave-safe bowl heat butter and marshmallows on HIGH for 3 minutes, stirring after 2 minutes. Stir until smooth. Follow steps 2, 3, and 4 above. Microwave cooking times may vary.

NUTRITION FACTS: Serving Size: 1 Snowman, undecorated (35g): Calories: 140; Calories from Fat: 25; Total Fat: 3g; Saturated Fat: 0.5g; Trans Fat: 0g; Cholesterol: 0mg; Sodium: 110mg; Total Carbohydrate: 27g; Dietary Fiber: 0g; Sugars: 13g; Protein: 1g.

Throw a Snowball-making Holiday Party!

To make *Rice Krispies Treats* that look like winter snowballs, start with the original recipe *(page 8)*. Let the cereal mixture cool slightly and divide into portions with a ½-cup measuring cup coated with cooking spray. With clean hands coated with butter, shape into balls. Roll in flaked coconut and sprinkle with powdered sugar.

Santa Faces Treats™

Preparation Time: 20 minutes / Total Time: 40 minutes / Servings: 12

Don't have time to do last-minute holiday baking? Make these quick snacks and your family and friends will rave about your creativity.

INGREDIENTS

3 tablespoons butter or margarine

1 package (10 oz., about 40) regular marshmallows
- *or* -
4 cups miniature marshmallows

6 cups *Rice Krispies* cereal

Canned frosting or decorating gel

Assorted candies

For best results, see our tips on page 8.

1. In large saucepan melt butter over low heat. Add marshmallows and stir until completely melted. Remove from heat.

2. Add KELLOGG'S RICE KRISPIES cereal. Stir until well coated.

3. Using buttered spatula or wax paper evenly press mixture into 15 x 10 x 1-inch pan coated with cooking spray. Cool slightly. Using 4-inch cookie cutter coated with cooking spray cut into Santa faces. Decorate with frosting and/or candies. Best if served the same day.

MICROWAVE DIRECTIONS: In microwave-safe bowl heat butter and marshmallows on HIGH for 3 minutes, stirring after 2 minutes. Stir until smooth. Follow steps 2 and 3 above. Microwave cooking times may vary.

NUTRITION FACTS: **Serving Size:** 1 Santa Face, undecorated (35g); Calories: 140; Calories from Fat: 25; **Total Fat:** 3g; **Saturated Fat:** 0.5g; Trans Fat: 0g; Cholesterol: 0mg; **Sodium:** 110mg; **Total Carbohydrate:** 27g; Dietary Fiber: 0g; Sugars: 13g; Protein: 1g.

Have a Merry Christmas with More Holiday Treats™!

During the holiday season, it's easy to find themed cookie cutters. In addition to the ideas on pages 48 to 61, look for these shapes.

- **Angels:** Use snowy white icing and silver or gold accents in decorating gel.
- **Bells:** Add touches of red, green, gold, or silver icing.
- **Bows:** Red and green are beautiful color choices.
- **Candles:** Use white or gold frosting, plus yellow for the flame.
- **Gingerbread Man:** A classic holiday shape.
- **Reindeer:** Decorate with frosting and candy—and give Rudolph a red nose!

Holiday Presents Treats™

Preparation Time: 20 minutes / Total Time: 40 minutes / Servings: 12

Easy-to-decorate stacks of the original squares *(page 8)* make delightful little gifts for family and friends.

INGREDIENTS

3 tablespoons butter or margarine

1 package (10 oz., about 40) regular marshmallows
- or -
4 cups miniature marshmallows

6 cups *Rice Krispies* cereal
- or -
6 cups *Cocoa Krispies* cereal

Canned frosting or decorating gel

Assorted candies

Red string licorice (optional)

For best results, see our tips on page 8.

1. In large saucepan melt butter over low heat. Add marshmallows and stir until completely melted. Remove from heat.

2. Add KELLOGG'S RICE KRISPIES cereal. Stir until well coated.

3. Using buttered spatula or wax paper evenly press mixture into 13 x 9 x 2-inch pan coated with cooking spray. Cool. Cut into 2-inch squares.

4. Use frosting to fasten stacks of two squares together. Decorate with additional frosting and/or candies. Tie bows on packages with licorice, if desired. Best if served the same day.

MICROWAVE DIRECTIONS: In microwave-safe bowl heat butter and marshmallows on HIGH for 3 minutes, stirring after 2 minutes. Stir until smooth. Follow steps 2, 3, and 4 above. Microwave cooking times may vary.

NUTRITION FACTS: Serving Size: 2 Squares (35g): Calories: 140; Calories from Fat: 25; Total Fat: 3g; Saturated Fat: 0.5g; Trans Fat: 0g; Cholesterol: 0mg; Sodium: 110mg; Total Carbohydrate: 27g; Dietary Fiber: 0g; Sugars: 13g; Protein: 1g.

Decorate Christmas Trees Good Enough to Eat!

Everyone, young and old alike, will enjoy decorating their own **Christmas Tree** *Treats* *(left)*. Start with the original *Rice Krispies Treats* recipe *(page 8)*, pressing the cereal mixture into a 15 x 10 x 1-inch pan. Use Christmas tree cookie cutters coated with cooking spray to cut out tree shapes. Decorate however you like with canned frosting, decorating gel, and assorted candies.

Rice Krispies Treats® Holiday House

Preparation Time: 3 hours 30 minutes / Total Time: 4 hours 30 minutes / Servings: 12

Unlike traditional ginger-bread houses, you don't have to do any baking to make this festive edible holiday decoration. Just follow the easy step-by-step instructions and photos to get beautiful results like you'll see in the photo on page 61.

INGREDIENTS

6 tablespoons butter or margarine, divided

2 packages (10 oz. each, about 80 total) regular marshmallows, divided
- *or* -
8 cups miniature marshmallows

12 cups *Rice Krispies* cereal (divided)
- *or* -
12 cups *Cocoa Krispies* cereal (divided)

Canned frosting or decorating gel

Assorted candies

For best results, see our tips on page 8.

1. In large saucepan melt 3 tablespoons of the butter over low heat. Add 1 package (10 ounces) of the marshmallows and stir until completely melted. Increase heat to medium. Cook and stir about 2 minutes more or until mixture starts to boil. Remove from heat.

2. Add 6 cups of the KELLOGG'S RICE KRISPIES cereal. Stir until well coated.

3. Using buttered spatula or wax paper evenly press mixture into 13 x 9 x 2-inch pan coated with cooking spray. Cool.

4. Repeat steps 1, 2, and 3 above using remaining butter, marshmallows and cereal, except press mixture into 15 x 10 x 1-inch pan coated with cooking spray. Cool.

5. To assemble house, place cereal mixture from 13 x 9 x 2-inch pan on foil-lined tray for base.

6. Cut the remaining pan of cereal mixture *(below)* into four 5 x 3½-inch rectangles for sides and ends of house and two 8 x 3-inch rectangles for roof. With one 5 x 3½-inch rectangle, laying vertically, cut off top corners at an angle to form peak of house. Repeat with second 5 x 3½-inch rectangle to form back of house. (Side walls, laying horizontally, should match bottom of angle cut in height.) Place the six pieces 1 inch apart on baking sheet coated with cooking spray. Bake at 250° F about 25 minutes. Remove from oven. Use spatula or knife to reshape pieces. Cool. Remove from pan.

7. Stand house front near center of base. Generously pipe frosting to attach house sides to back of house front *(below)*.

continued on next page

Holiday House - continued

8. Use frosting to attach house back and roof pieces. Use leftover pieces of cereal mixture to make chimney and trees, and attach with frosting *(left)*.

9. Decorate house with additional frosting and candies, using frosting to attach candies to house *(below)*.

MICROWAVE DIRECTIONS: In microwave-safe bowl heat butter and marshmallows on HIGH for 3 minutes, stirring after 2 minutes. Stir until smooth. Follow steps 2 through 9. Microwave cooking times may vary.

NUTRITION FACTS: Serving Size: ¹/₁₂ House (71g): Calories: 270; Calories from Fat: 50; Total Fat: 6g; Saturated Fat: 1g; Trans Fat: 0g; Cholesterol: 0mg; Sodium: 220mg; Total Carbohydrate: 54g; Dietary Fiber: 0g; Sugars: 26g; Protein: 3g.

Hanukkah Treats™

Preparation Time: 20 minutes / Total Time: 40 minutes / Servings: 12

Look for Hanukkah-themed cookie cutters to shape and decorate the original recipe *(page 8)* for one of the eight nights of celebration.

INGREDIENTS

3 tablespoons butter or margarine

1 package (10 oz., about 40) regular marshmallows

- or -

4 cups miniature marshmallows

6 cups *Rice Krispies* cereal

Canned frosting

Assorted candies

For best results, and to substitute marshmallow crème for the marshmallows, see our tips on page 8.

1. In large saucepan melt butter over low heat. Add marshmallows and stir until completely melted. Remove from heat.

2. Add KELLOGG'S RICE KRISPIES cereal. Stir until well coated.

3. Using buttered spatula or wax paper evenly press mixture into 15 x 10 x 1-inch pan coated with cooking spray. Cool slightly. Using cookie cutters coated with cooking spray, cut into Hanukkah-inspired shapes *(see sidebar below)*. Decorate with frosting and/or candies. Best if served the same day.

MICROWAVE DIRECTIONS: In microwave-safe bowl heat butter and marshmallows on HIGH for 3 minutes, stirring after 2 minutes. Stir until smooth. Follow steps 2 and 3 above. Microwave cooking times may vary.

NUTRITION FACTS: Serving Size: 1 cookie cutter shape, undecorated (35g): Calories: 140; Calories from Fat: 25; Total Fat: 3g; Saturated Fat: 0.5g; Trans Fat: 0g; Cholesterol: 0mg; Sodium: 110mg; Total Carbohydrate: 27g; Dietary Fiber: 0g; Sugars: 13g; Protein: 1g.

Light Up Your Hanukkah Celebration!

The Jewish Festival of Lights is celebrated for eight evenings in late fall or early winter with lighting candles, exchanging gifts and foil-wrapped chocolate coins, singing songs, and playing games. All of the following shapes, shown in the photo, make great inspirations for *Treats* decorated in blue and white with hints of yellow.

- **Dreidl:** The four-sided top traditionally spun in a simple, lively Hanukkah game.
- **Menorah:** The candelabrum holds eight candles plus another to light them.
- **Star of David:** Jewish six-pointed star.
- **Torah:** The Hebrew Bible, written on a scroll that is unrolled for reading.

Kwanzaa Treats™

Preparation Time: 20 minutes / Total Time: 40 minutes / Servings: 12

It's so easy and so much fun to make and decorate the original recipe *(page 8)* in celebration of family, community, and culture.

INGREDIENTS

3 tablespoons butter or margarine

1 package (10 oz., about 40) regular marshmallows

- or -

4 cups miniature marshmallows

6 cups *Rice Krispies* cereal

Canned frosting

Assorted candies

For best results, see our tips on page 8.

1. In large saucepan melt butter over low heat. Add marshmallows and stir until completely melted. Remove from heat.

2. Add KELLOGG'S RICE KRISPIES cereal. Stir until well coated.

3. Using buttered spatula or wax paper evenly press mixture into 15 x 10 x 1-inch pan coated with cooking spray. Cool slightly. Using cookie cutters coated with cooking spray or stencils cut from sturdy cardboard, cut into Kwanzaa-inspired shapes *(see sidebar below)*. Decorate with frosting and/or candies. Best if served the same day.

MICROWAVE DIRECTIONS: In microwave-safe bowl heat butter and marshmallows on HIGH for 3 minutes, stirring after 2 minutes. Stir until smooth. Follow steps 2 and 3 above. Microwave cooking times may vary.

NUTRITION FACTS: Serving Size: 1 cookie cutter shape, undecorated (35g): Calories: 140; Calories from Fat: 25; Total Fat: 3g; Saturated Fat: 0.5g; Trans Fat: 0g; Cholesterol: 0mg; Sodium: 110mg; Total Carbohydrate: 27g; Dietary Fiber: 0g; Sugars: 13g; Protein: 1g.

Harvest Happy Family Times!

Inspired by ancient African harvest celebrations, Kwanzaa is observed from December 26 through January 1. The name comes from Swahili for "first fruits," and the earth's bounty is one of the inspirations for easy-to-make **Kwanzaa** *Treats*.

- **Fruits and Vegetables:** Use cookie cutters or stencils to cut out fruit or vegetables.
- **Kwanzaa Flags:** A banner with horizontal stripes of red, black, and green is the official Kwanzaa holiday flag, easy to make with frosting on rectangular shapes.
- **Candles:** Cut out candle shapes and frost them in red, black, and green.
- **Presents:** Make **Holiday Presents** *(page 56)*, giving them Kwanzaa colors.

Soccer Ball and Baseball Treats™

Preparation Time: 20 minutes / Total Time: 40 minutes / Servings: 12

Need a snack for after the big game? These easy-to-prepare sports-themed shapes will be a big hit.

INGREDIENTS

3 tablespoons butter or margarine

1 package (10 oz., about 40) regular marshmallows

- or -

4 cups miniature marshmallows

6 cups *Rice Krispies* cereal

Canned frosting and/or decorating gel

For best results, see our tips on page 8.

1. In large saucepan melt butter over low heat. Add marshmallows and stir until completely melted. Remove from heat.

2. Add KELLOGG'S RICE KRISPIES cereal. Stir until well coated.

3. Using buttered spatula or wax paper evenly press mixture into 15 x 10 x 1-inch pan coated with cooking spray. Cool slightly. Using 2-inch round cookie cutter coated with cooking spray cut into circles. Decorate with frosting to make baseballs and soccer balls. Best if served the same day.

MICROWAVE DIRECTIONS: In microwave-safe bowl heat butter and marshmallows on HIGH for 3 minutes, stirring after 2 minutes. Stir until smooth. Follow steps 2 and 3 above. Microwave cooking times may vary.

NUTRITION FACTS: **Serving Size:** 2 Balls (35g): **Calories:** 140; Calories from Fat: 25; **Total Fat:** 3g; **Saturated Fat:** 0.5g; **Trans Fat:** 0g; **Cholesterol:** 0mg; **Sodium:** 110mg; **Total Carbohydrate:** 27g; **Dietary Fiber:** 0g; **Sugars:** 13g; **Protein:** 1g.

After School Is Time to Snacktivate!

After-school snack time is a great opportunity for good nutrition and family fun.

- **Plan It:** Designate specific snack times as part of your family's routine.
- **Pick It:** Keep snacks small, simple, pre-portioned, and nutritious. Eat a variety from the primary food groups.
- **Make It:** Let kids join in preparing snacks, like making *Rice Krispies Treats*.
- **Move It:** Keep active so that the energy (calories) you take in equals the calories you burn off through physical activity. Energy balance is key to healthy living.

Chocolate Nutty Mini-Footballs

Preparation Time: 20 minutes / Total Time: 40 minutes / Servings: 16

For game day or an after-practice snack, make this classic mixture and shape it into miniature footballs.

INGREDIENTS

3 tablespoons butter or margarine

1 package (10 oz., about 40) regular marshmallows

- or -

4 cups miniature marshmallows

½ cup peanut butter

6 cups *Cocoa Krispies* cereal

Canned frosting or decorating gel

For best results, see our tips on page 8.

1. In large saucepan melt butter over low heat. Add marshmallows and stir until completely melted. Remove from heat. Stir in peanut butter until melted.

2. Add KELLOGG'S COCOA KRISPIES cereal. Stir until well coated.

3. Cool slightly. Using buttered hands shape mixture into sixteen 3-inch footballs. Decorate with frosting. Best if served the same day.

MICROWAVE DIRECTIONS: In microwave-safe bowl heat butter and marshmallows on HIGH for 3 minutes, stirring after 2 minutes. Stir until smooth. Add peanut butter, stirring until melted. Follow steps 2 and 3 above. Microwave cooking times may vary.

NUTRITION FACTS: Serving Size: 1 Mini-Football (40g): Calories: 170; Calories from Fat: 60; Total Fat: 7g; Saturated Fat: 1.5g; Trans Fat: 0g; Cholesterol: 0mg; Sodium: 135mg; Total Carbohydrate: 27g; Dietary Fiber: less than 1g; Sugars: 15g; Protein: 3g.

Score with Other Sports-themed Snacks!

It's easy and fun to make sport-inspired *Treats* for a winning after-play snack.

- **Basketball:** Cut out circles. Decorate with orange-colored frosting and black gel.
- **Bowling:** With cutters or stencils, cut out bowling balls and pins and decorate.
- **Running:** Use a stencil to cut out the shapes of running shoes. Add licorice laces.
- **Tennis:** Cut out round balls and frost in bright yellow. Use a cardboard stencil to cut racquets; frost them and use decorating gel to add the strings.
- **Trophies:** Look for trophy-shaped cutters or make stencils. Cover in gold frosting and use decorating gel to write on the names of team members. Everyone wins!

Peanut Butter and Jelly Crisps

Preparation Time: 20 minutes / Total Time: 40 minutes / Servings: 12

Spread your favorite jelly or jam between layers of cereal mixture infused with creamy peanut butter to make this crispy version of a classic PB&J sandwich.

INGREDIENTS

3 tablespoons butter or margarine

1 package (10 oz., about 40) regular marshmallows
- or -
4 cups miniature marshmallows

⅓ cup creamy peanut butter

6 cups *Rice Krispies* cereal

⅓ cup desired flavor jelly

For best results, see our tips on page 8.

1. In large saucepan melt butter over low heat. Add marshmallows and stir until completely melted. Remove from heat. Stir in peanut butter until melted.

2. Add KELLOGG'S RICE KRISPIES cereal. Stir until well coated.

3. Using buttered spatula or wax paper evenly press half of the cereal mixture into 8 x 8 x 2-inch pan coated with cooking spray. Spread with jelly. Press remaining cereal mixture on top. Cool. Cut into 2-inch squares. Best if served the same day.

MICROWAVE DIRECTIONS: In microwave-safe bowl heat butter and marshmallows on HIGH for 3 minutes, stirring after 2 minutes. Stir until smooth. Add peanut butter, stirring until melted. Follow steps 2 and 3 above. Microwave cooking times may vary.

NUTRITION FACTS: Serving Size: 2 Squares (39g): Calories: 150; Calories from Fat: 25; Total Fat: 3g; Saturated Fat: 0.5g; Trans Fat: 0g; Cholesterol: 0mg; Sodium: 160mg; Total Carbohydrate: 30g; Dietary Fiber: 0g; Sugars: 16g; Protein: 1g.

Ring the Changes on an After-School Favorite!

Even a simple combination like peanut butter and jelly gives you the chance to come up with endless yummy variations.

- **Swap Out the Jelly:** Instead of the strawberry jam shown here, use another jam or jelly you like, such as apricot, peach, grape, blueberry, raspberry, or marmalade.
- **Try Different Nut Butters:** Look in supermarkets and health foods stores for spreads made from other nuts, including almonds, cashews, and macadamia nuts.
- **Add Mix-ins:** Along with the *Rice Krispies* cereal, stir in raisins or chocolate chips.

Gold Medal Sundae

Preparation Time: 15 minutes / Total Time: 35 minutes / Servings: 12

Use golden rounds of the original recipe *(page 8)* as bases for sundaes that make everyone feel like they're on the winner's stand.

INGREDIENTS

3 tablespoons butter or margarine

1 package (10 oz., about 40) regular marshmallows

- or -

4 cups miniature marshmallows

6 cups *Rice Krispies* cereal

3 cups frozen fat-free vanilla yogurt

¾ cup strawberry ice cream topping

1½ cups frozen nondairy whipped topping, thawed

12 maraschino cherries, drained

For best results, see our tips on page 8.

1. In large saucepan melt butter over low heat. Add marshmallows and stir until completely melted. Remove from heat.

2. Add KELLOGG'S RICE KRISPIES cereal. Stir until well coated.

3. Using buttered spatula or wax paper evenly press mixture into 15 x 10 x 1-inch pan coated with cooking spray. Cool.

4. Cut into rounds, using 3-inch cookie cutter. Top each round with frozen yogurt. Drizzle with ice cream topping. Dollop with whipped topping and top with cherry. Serve immediately.

In microwave-safe bowl heat butter   and marshmallows on HIGH for 3 minutes, stirring after 2 minutes. Stir until smooth. Follow steps 2, 3, and 4 above. Microwave cooking times may vary.

Serving Size: Calories: Calories from Fat: Total Fat: Saturated Fat: Trans Fat: Cholesterol: Sodium: Total Carbohydrate: Dietary Fiber: Sugars: Protein:

Have a Cool Time Dreaming Up Your Own Sundaes!

Enjoy more special desserts by using *Rice Krispies Treats* in other sundaes.

- **Banana Split** *Treats*: Add a scoop of ice cream, sliced banana, bottled strawberry or pineapple topping, and slivered almonds.
- **Peppermint-Chocolate Sundaes:** Top a round with mint or mint-chip ice cream or frozen yogurt and a drizzle of chocolate sauce.
- **Tropical Sundae** *Treats*: Dip into some pineapple sherbet or frozen yogurt, drizzle with coconut syrup, and sprinkle with coconut shreds.

Crunchy Ice Cream Sandwiches

Preparation Time: 15 minutes / Total Time: 15 minutes / Servings: 12

Nothing cools you off more deliciously on a hot summer day than one of these easy-to-assemble, peanutty ice cream sandwiches.

INGREDIENTS

3 tablespoons butter or margarine

30 regular marshmallows
- *or* -
3 cups miniature marshmallows

½ cup creamy peanut butter

4 cups *Rice Krispies* cereal
- *or* -
4 cups *Cocoa Krispies* cereal

2 cups ice cream, softened

For best results, see our tips on page 8.

1. In large saucepan melt butter over low heat. Add marshmallows and stir until completely melted. Remove from heat. Stir in peanut butter.

2. Add KELLOGG'S RICE KRISPIES cereal. Stir until well coated.

3. Using buttered spatula or wax paper evenly press mixture into 13 x 9 x 2-inch pan coated with cooking spray. Cool. Cut into twelve 3-inch squares.

4. Top six of the cereal squares with ice cream. Place remaining squares on top. Cut each in half, making twelve 3 x 1½-inch sandwiches. Individually wrap in plastic wrap. Store in airtight container in freezer for up to 6 weeks.

MICROWAVE DIRECTIONS: In microwave-safe bowl heat butter and marshmallows on HIGH for 3 minutes, stirring after 2 minutes. Stir until smooth. Add peanut butter, stirring until melted. Follow steps 2, 3, and 4 above. Microwave cooking times may vary.

NUTRITION FACTS: **Serving Size:** 1 Sandwich (60g); **Calories:** 220; Calories from Fat: 100; **Total Fat:** 11g; **Saturated Fat:** 3g; **Trans Fat:** 0.5g; **Cholesterol:** 10mg; **Sodium:** 140mg; **Total Carbohydrate:** 28g; **Dietary Fiber:** less than 1g; **Sugars:** 16g; **Protein:** 4g.

Chill Out with More Ice Cream Sandwiches!

Use the ice cream sandwiches recipe on this page as just the starting point for your own *Rice Krispies Treats* creations. Here are some ideas to get you started.

- **Go Back to Basics:** Replace the cereal mixture here with the original recipe *(page 8)*.
- **Go Wild:** Use other *Treats* mixtures you like in this book, or your own variations.
- **Swap Out the Filling:** Try your own favorite ice cream, frozen yogurt, or sorbet.
- **Dip Them:** Dip half of each sandwich in melted chocolate *(see page 31)*.

Chocolate Scotcheroos

Preparation Time: 20 minutes / Total Time: 20 minutes / Servings: 24

Corn syrup, sugar, and peanut butter replace the usual marshmallows and butter in this popular variation. Before measuring the syrup, coat the cup with cooking spray, and the syrup will pour out easily.

INGREDIENTS

1 cup light corn syrup

1 cup sugar

1 cup peanut butter

6 cups *Rice Krispies* cereal
-or-
6 cups *Cocoa Krispies* cereal

1 package (6 oz., 1 cup) semisweet chocolate morsels

1 cup butterscotch chips

For best results, see our tips on page 8.

1. Place corn syrup and sugar into 3-quart saucepan. Cook over medium heat, stirring frequently, until sugar dissolves and mixture begins to boil. Remove from heat. Stir in peanut butter. Mix well. Add KELLOGG'S RICE KRISPIES cereal. Stir until well coated. Press mixture into 13 x 9 x 2-inch pan coated with cooking spray. Set aside.

2. Melt chocolate and butterscotch chips together in 1-quart saucepan over low heat, stirring constantly. Spread evenly over cereal mixture. Let stand until firm. Cut into 2 x 1-inch bars when cool.

NUTRITION FACTS: **Serving Size:** 2 Bars (56g); **Calories:** 240; Calories from Fat: 90; **Total Fat:** 10g; **Saturated Fat:** 4.5g; **Trans Fat:** 0g; **Cholesterol:** 0mg; **Sodium:** 115mg; **Total Carbohydrate:** 38g; **Dietary Fiber:** less than 1g; **Sugars:** 23g; **Protein:** 3g.

join the
CRISPNESS CHORUS

Stir Up Some Spins on Scotcheroos!

If you love the rich taste of the Scotcheroos chocolate-butterscotch topping, try spreading it on top of other favorite *Rice Krispies Treats* in this book. You might also enjoy other variations on the recipe's mixture. *(Look in specialty foods stores or online for harder-to-find flavors.)*

- **Milky Scotcheroos:** Use milk-chocolate morsels in place of semisweet.
- **White Chocolate Scotcheroos:** Replace the semisweet chocolate morsels with white chocolate morsels.
- **Cinnaroos:** Substitute cinnamon-flavored baking chips.
- **Mintyroos:** In place of the butterscotch chips, use mint-flavored baking morsels.
- **Razzaroos:** Look for raspberry-flavored baking chips to replace the butterscotch.

Chocolate Yummies

Preparation Time: 20 minutes / Total Time: 1 hour 20 minutes / Servings: 12

These snacks combine all the flavors of classic s'mores with a touch of peanut butter.

INGREDIENTS

7 rectangular sheets Keebler® Grahams crackers (each cracker sheet measures about 5 × 2 inches and is scored into 4 pieces)

2½ cups miniature marshmallows

1 package (12 oz., 2 cups) semisweet chocolate morsels

⅔ cup light corn syrup

3 tablespoons butter or margarine

½ cup crunchy peanut butter

3 cups *Rice Krispies* cereal

For best results, see our tips on page 8.

Make S'More S'Mores!

For **S'Mores** *Treats*, start with the original recipe *(page 8)*, but use *Cocoa Krispies* cereal. Along with the cereal, add ¾ cup graham crackers broken into ½-inch pieces. After pressing into the pan, sprinkle with ½ cup miniature marshmallows and ¼ cup miniature semisweet chocolate chips. Cut into squares when cool.

1. Coat 13 x 9 x 2-inch microwave-safe dish with cooking spray. Arrange KEEBLER GRAHAMS crackers in single layer in dish, breaking crackers as needed to fit. Sprinkle marshmallows evenly over crackers.

2. Microwave on HIGH 1 minute or until marshmallows are puffy. Remove from microwave. Cool completely.

3. In 2-quart microwave-safe mixing bowl combine chocolate morsels, corn syrup and butter. Microwave on HIGH about 1½ minutes or until chocolate is melted, stirring every 30 seconds. Stir in peanut butter. Add KELLOGG'S RICE KRISPIES cereal, mixing until combined.

4. Spread evenly over marshmallows. Cover and refrigerate about 1 hour or until firm. Cut and store in airtight container in refrigerator.

CONVENTIONAL DIRECTIONS: Follow step 1 using ovenproof baking dish. Bake at 375°F about 7 minutes, until marshmallows are puffy. Cool completely. In medium saucepan combine chocolate, corn syrup and butter. Stir constantly over medium-low heat until melted. Remove from heat. Stir in peanut butter. Stir in KELLOGG'S RICE KRISPIES cereal. Complete as in step 4 above.

NUTRITION FACTS: **Serving Size:** 1 piece (32g): **Calories:** 140; Calories from Fat: 60; **Total Fat:** 7g; **Saturated Fat:** 3.5g; **Trans Fat:** 0g; **Cholesterol:** 5mg; **Sodium:** 55mg; **Total Carbohydrate:** 21g; **Dietary Fiber:** less than 1g; **Sugars:** 13g; **Protein:** 2g.

Crunchy Fudge Sandwiches

Preparation Time: 20 minutes / Total Time: 30 minutes / Servings: 25

A rich fudge layer separates two crispy layers made with butterscotch morsels and peanut butter.

INGREDIENTS

1 cup butterscotch morsels

½ cup peanut butter

4 cups *Rice Krispies* cereal

1 package (6 oz.) semisweet chocolate morsels

½ cup powdered sugar

2 tablespoons butter or margarine, softened

1 tablespoon water

For best results, see our tips on page 8.

1. Melt butterscotch morsels with peanut butter in heavy saucepan over very low heat, stirring constantly until well blended. Remove from heat.

2. Add KELLOGG'S RICE KRISPIES cereal to butterscotch mixture, stirring until well coated. Press half of cereal mixture into 8 x 8 x 2-inch pan coated with cooking spray. Chill in refrigerator while preparing filling. Set remaining cereal mixture aside.

3. Combine chocolate morsels, powdered sugar, butter and water. Stir over very low heat until chocolate melts and mixture is well blended. Spread over chilled cereal mixture. Spread remaining cereal mixture evenly over top. Press in gently. Chill. Remove from refrigerator for about 10 minutes before cutting into squares.

NUTRITION FACTS: Serving Size: 1 piece (29g); Calories: 140; Calories from Fat: 70; Total Fat: 8g; Saturated Fat: 4.5g; Trans Fat: 0g; Cholesterol: 0mg; Sodium: 60mg; Total Carbohydrate: 17g; Dietary Fiber: less than 1g; Sugars: 12g; Protein: 2g.

Spread the Fun with More Fudgy Treats™!

Have fun dreaming up your own **Crunchy Fudge Sandwich** variations.

- **Use Fudge Sauce:** Replace the mixture of chocolate morsels, powdered sugar, butter, and water with store-bought fudge sauce right out of the jar.
- **Try Other Chips:** Replace the semisweet with milk or white chocolate morsels.
- **Add Flavorings:** When making the fudge, use 2 teaspoons of the water plus 1 teaspoon of a bottled flavoring extract like vanilla or banana.

Caramel Cashew Crunch Bars

Preparation Time: 10 minutes / Total Time: 10 minutes / Servings: 24

Featuring melted caramels in place of the marshmallows, these easy snacks deliver all the crunchy satisfaction of a great candy bar.

INGREDIENTS

1 bag (14 oz.) caramels (wrappers removed)

2 tablespoons margarine

2 tablespoons water

6 cups *Cocoa Krispies* cereal

1 cup cashews

1 cup white chocolate chips (divided)

For best results, see our tips on page 8.

1. In large microwave-safe mixing bowl, microwave caramels, margarine and water at HIGH 3 minutes or until melted and smooth, stirring after each minute.

2. Add KELLOGG'S COCOA KRISPIES cereal and cashews. Stir until well coated. Add ½ cup white chocolate chips, stirring until combined.

3. Spread mixture into 13 x 9 x 2-inch pan coated with cooking spray. Let stand about 2 minutes. Sprinkle the remaining white chocolate chips over the mixture and press evenly into the pan. Cut into 2-inch squares when cool.

NUTRITION FACTS: Serving Size: 1 Bar (44g): Calories: 200; Calories from Fat: 70: Total Fat: 8g: Saturated Fat: 3.5g: Trans Fat: 0g: Cholesterol: 0mg: Sodium: 110mg: Total Carbohydrate: 30g: Dietary Fiber: 0g; Sugars: 20g: Protein: 2g.

Crunch Your Way Through More Delicious Bars

Each of the main ingredients in **Caramel Cashew Crunch Bars** gives you the chance to play with the recipe and make your own irresistible versions.

- **Try Different Caramel Flavors:** Look for those flavored with chocolate, maple, mocha, and ginger, to name a few.
- **Swap Out Cereals:** Instead of *Cocoa Krispies* cereal, use *Rice Krispies* cereal or a mixture of the two.
- **Mix Up the Nuts:** Try peanuts, pecans, macadamias, walnuts, or hazelnuts.
- **Go Wild with the Chocolate:** Use milk chocolate, semisweet, or a mixture.

Rice Krispies Treats® Caterpillars

Preparation Time: 20 minutes / Total Time: 40 minutes / Servings: 12

For the pretty centerpiece of a springtime party, create caterpillars from cut-out rounds of the original recipe *(page 8)*, then decorate with pastel frosting and candies.

INGREDIENTS

3 tablespoons butter or margarine

1 package (10 oz., about 40) regular marshmallows
- or -
4 cups miniature marshmallows

6 cups *Rice Krispies* cereal

Canned frosting or decorating gel

Assorted candies

For best results, see our tips on page 8.

1. In large saucepan melt butter over low heat. Add marshmallows and stir until completely melted. Remove from heat.

2. Add KELLOGG'S RICE KRISPIES cereal. Stir until well coated.

3. Using buttered spatula or wax paper evenly press mixture into 15 x 10 x 1-inch pan coated with cooking spray. Cool slightly. Using small round cookie cutters coated with cooking spray cut out about 100 circles.

4. Place eight or nine circles next to each other to form each caterpillar. Decorate with frosting and/or candies. Best if served the same day.

MICROWAVE DIRECTIONS: In microwave-safe bowl heat butter and marshmallows on HIGH for 3 minutes, stirring after 2 minutes. Stir until smooth. Follow steps 2, 3, and 4 above. Microwave cooking times may vary.

NUTRITION FACTS: **Serving Size:** 1 Caterpillar (44g): **Calories:** 140; **Calories from Fat:** 25; **Total Fat:** 3g; **Saturated Fat:** 0.5g; **Trans Fat:** 0g; **Cholesterol:** 0mg; **Sodium:** 110mg; **Total Carbohydrate:** 27g; **Dietary Fiber:** 0g; **Sugars:** 13g; **Protein:** 1g.

Try Other Springtime Party Snacks!

Rice Krispies Treats **Fun Balls** *(left)* are wonderful for a spring afternoon party. Make the original recipe *(page 8)*. Using a ½-cup measuring cup coated with cooking spray, divide the warm cereal mixture into portions. Then, using clean hands coated with butter, shape each portion into a ball. Insert wooden ice cream sticks and decorate with coconut, colored sprinkles, or melted chocolate. Let stand until firm.

Rice Krispies Treats® Pizza

Preparation Time: 15 minutes / Total Time: 35 minutes / Servings: 12

Everybody loves a pizza party. This dessert version will be the hit of slumber parties and picnics alike.

INGREDIENTS

3 tablespoons butter or margarine

1 package (10 oz., about 40) regular marshmallows
- or -
4 cups miniature marshmallows

6 cups *Rice Krispies* cereal
- or -
6 cups *Cocoa Krispies* cereal

Strawberry jam

Canned frosting

Fruit roll-ups, cut into 1¼-inch circles

Multicolored sprinkles

For best results, see our tips on page 8.

1. In large saucepan melt butter over low heat. Add marshmallows and stir until completely melted. Remove from heat.

2. Add KELLOGG'S RICE KRISPIES cereal. Stir until well coated.

3. Using buttered spatula or wax paper evenly press mixture into 12-inch pizza pan coated with cooking spray. Cool.

4. Spread strawberry jam on top for "tomato sauce." Carefully spread frosting over jam for "cheese." Add fruit roll-up circles for "pepperoni." Top with sprinkles. Cut into slices to serve. Best if served the same day.

MICROWAVE DIRECTIONS: In microwave-safe bowl heat butter and marshmallows on HIGH for 3 minutes, stirring after 2 minutes. Stir until smooth. Follow steps 2, 3, and 4 above. Microwave cooking times may vary.

NUTRITION FACTS: **Serving Size:** 1 Pizza Slice (34g); **Calories:** 140; **Calories from Fat:** 25; **Total Fat:** 3g; **Saturated Fat:** 0.5g; **Trans Fat:** 0g; **Cholesterol:** 0mg; **Sodium:** 110mg; **Total Carbohydrate:** 27g; **Dietary Fiber:** 0g; **Sugars:** 13g; **Protein:** 1g.

Fool Your Friends with More Rice Krispies Treats® in Disguise!

It's easy to transform the original recipe *(page 8)* into other fun foods.
- **Mini-Burgers:** Mold buns from a mixture made with *Rice Krispies* cereal and burgers from a batch made with *Cocoa Krispies* cereal.
- **Piggies-in-Blankets:** Mold mini hot dogs from a cereal mixture tinted pink with a little red food coloring. Wrap in blankets of uncolored cereal mixture.
- **Sushi** *Treats:* Mold small rectangles of sushi rice from some of the original mixture; color the melted marshmallows for part of the batch with a little red food coloring and mold into thin rectangles for the fish that goes on top.

Birthday Fun Cups

Preparation Time: 20 minutes / Total Time: 40 minutes / Servings: 16

Patted into muffin cups, everybody's favorite marshmallow-and-cereal snacks make great crusts for individual tarts. Fill with pudding, ice cream, or frozen yogurt.

INGREDIENTS

3 tablespoons butter or margarine

1 package (10 oz., about 40) regular marshmallows
- or -
4 cups miniature marshmallows

6 cups *Rice Krispies* cereal
- or -
6 cups *Cocoa Krispies* cereal

Pudding, ice cream or frozen yogurt

Ice cream topping, whipped topping and/or chopped nuts (optional)

For best results, see our tips on page 8.

1. In large saucepan melt butter over low heat. Add marshmallows and stir until completely melted. Remove from heat.

2. Add KELLOGG'S RICE KRISPIES cereal. Stir until well coated.

3. Divide warm mixture into sixteen 2½-inch muffin-pan cups coated with cooking spray. Shape mixture into individual cups. Cool. Remove from pans.

4. Before serving fill with pudding, ice cream or frozen yogurt. Top with ice cream topping, whipped topping or nuts, if desired. Serve immediately.

MICROWAVE DIRECTIONS: In microwave-safe bowl heat butter and marshmallows on HIGH for 3 minutes, stirring after 2 minutes. Stir until smooth. Follow steps 2, 3, and 4 above. Microwave cooking times may vary.

NUTRITION FACTS: Serving Size: 1 Birthday Cup, unfilled (27g): Calories: 100; Calories from Fat: 20; Total Fat: 2g; Saturated Fat: 0g; Trans Fat: 0g; Cholesterol: 0mg; Sodium: 80mg; Total Carbohydrate: 20g; Dietary Fiber: 0g; Sugars: 10g; Protein: 1g.

Surprise Someone with a Personal Rice Krispies Treats® Cake!

It's easy to make a **Special Occasion Cake** from *Rice Krispies Treats*. Prepare the cereal mixture for the original recipe *(page 8)* or for any other recipe you like. Using a buttered spatula or wax paper, press the mixture into two 9-inch round cake pans lined with foil and coated with cooking spray. Cool. Unmold, remove the foil, and make 2 single-layer cakes or stack with frosting for a double-layer cake, decorating with frosting and candies. Don't forget the candles!

Rice Krispies Treats® Wedding Cake

Preparation Time: 4 hours / Total Time: 5 hours / Servings: 76

Many engaged couples discover that both of them have had a lifelong love of America's favorite snack. So, what better way could there be to have a fun wedding cake that everyone will enjoy? It takes some time to prepare all the layers, but each is as easy to make as the original recipe *(page 8)*. For a smaller wedding, a make-believe party for kids, just make and decorate fewer, smaller layers.

INGREDIENTS

28½ tablespoons (3 sticks plus 1½ tablespoons) butter or margarine, divided

9½ packages (10 oz each, about 380 total) regular marshmallows, divided

- or -

38 cups miniature marshmallows

57 cups *Rice Krispies* cereal (divided)

Canned frosting or decorating gel

Edible flowers, for decoration (optional, see note)

For best results, see our tips on page 8.

1. In a large pot melt 9 tablespoons butter over low heat. Add 3 packages (30 ounces) marshmallows and stir until completely melted. Remove from heat.

2. Add 18 cups KELLOGG'S RICE KRISPIES cereal. Stir until well coated.

3. Using buttered spatula or clean buttered hands, evenly press mixture into 14 x 2-inch round cake pan coated with cooking spray and lined with parchment paper. Unmold and let cool.

4. Meanwhile, in a large pot melt 7½ tablespoons butter over low heat. Add 2½ packages (25 ounces) marshmallows and stir until completely melted. Remove from heat.

5. Add 15 cups KELLOGG'S RICE KRISPIES cereal. Stir until well coated.

6. Using buttered spatula or clean buttered hands, evenly press mixture into 12 x 2-inch round cake pan coated with cooking spray and lined with parchment paper. Unmold and let cool.

7. Meanwhile, in a large pot melt 6 tablespoons butter over low heat. Add 2 packages (20 ounces) marshmallows and stir until completely melted. Remove from heat.

8. Add 12 cups KELLOGG'S RICE KRISPIES cereal. Stir until well coated.

9. Using buttered spatula or clean buttered hands evenly press mixture into 10 x 2-inch round cake pan coated with cooking spray and lined with parchment paper. Unmold and let cool.

10. Meanwhile, in a large pot melt 4½ tablespoons butter over low heat. Add 1½ packages (15 ounces) marshmallows and stir until completely melted. Remove from heat.

11. Add 9 cups KELLOGG'S RICE KRISPIES cereal. Stir until well coated.

12. Using buttered spatula or clean buttered hands evenly press mixture into 8 x 2-inch round cake pan coated with cooking spray and lined with parchment paper *(right)*. Unmold and let cool.

13. Meanwhile, in a large pot melt 1½ tablespoons butter over low heat. Add ½ package (5 ounces) marshmallows and stir until completely melted. Remove from heat.

14. Add 3 cups KELLOGG'S RICE KRISPIES cereal. Stir until well coated.

15. Using buttered spatula or clean buttered hands evenly press mixture into 6 x 2-inch cake pan coated with cooking spray and lined with parchment paper. Unmold and let cool.

16. Once all layers have cooled, stack them carefully centered on top of each other from largest on the bottom to smallest on top *(left)*.

continued on next page

Wedding Cake - continued

17. Using a tube of frosting or decorating gel and a decorative tip, pipe ribbons or garlands and small flower shapes or dots all along the sides of the layers *(left)*.

18. Add edible flowers around the sides or on top.

19. To serve, use a serrated bread knife to cut the top layer only into servings *(see sidebar)*. Continue to cut and serve the cake layer by layer.

NUTRITION FACTS: **Serving Size:** 1 Slice, unfrosted (35g); **Calories:** 140; **Calories from Fat:** 25; **Total Fat:** 3g; **Saturated Fat:** 0.5g; **Trans Fat:** 0g; **Cholesterol:** 0mg; **Sodium:** 110mg; **Total Carbohydrate:** 27g; **Dietary Fiber:** 0g; **Sugars:** 13g; **Protein:** 1g.

SERVINGS PER LAYER:

Layer size	Number of servings
6-inch	6 to 8
8-inch	8 to 10
10-inch	10 to 15
12-inch	15 to 20
14-inch	25 to 30

A Natural Decoration for Your Cake

In addition to frosting decorations, look in supermarket produce sections for edible flowers such as marigolds, carnations, hibiscus, nasturtiums, peonies, roses, or violets. Be careful to use only those grown without pesticides or chemicals.

Index

weldon**owen**

415 Jackson Street, Suite 200, San Francisco, CA 94111
Telephone: 415 291 0100   Fax: 415 291 8841
www.wopublishing.com

Paperback edition first printed in 2011
Printed in the USA

10 9 8 7 6 5 4 3 2

2011   2012   2013   2014

Library of Congress Cataloging-in-Publication Data is available.

ISBN 13: 978-1-61628-119-9

Weldon Owen is a division of
BONNIER

Project Editor/Writer Norman Kolpas

Proofreader Brenda Koplin

Designer Jason Budow

Photography Carin Krasner
Photos appear on the cover, front and back endpapers, and pages 8, 9, 10, 11, 17, 21, 22, 25, 26, 42, 46, 50, 54, 57, 59, 60, 61, 62, 65, 70, 91, 92, and 93

Food Stylist Marah Abel

Food Stylist Assistant Rebecca Farr

Prop Stylist Kristina Rodgers

Rice Krispies Treats Wedding Cake (pages 90-93)   developed by Marah Abel.

Models Tyler Budow and Caden Budow

All other images and photographs appear under license and with permission of the Kellogg North America Company.

The following trademarks and characters are used with permission of the Kellogg Company:
COCOA KRISPIES®, KEEBLER®, RICE KRISPIES®,   RICE KRISPIES TREATS®, SNAP!™, CRACKLE!™, POP!™ CHILDHOOD IS CALLING!™

www.shopkelloggs.com